The Cross Series

CrossWalk

Vital Steps in Your Walk with God
Expanded Edition

Sherri and Scott Dalton

Hikanos Press

CrossWalk
Vital Steps in Your Walk with God
Expanded Edition

Book 1 of the "Cross" Series of discipleship and training materials.

Hikanos Press
113 Paramus Ave.
Newark, OH 43055

ISBN 13: 978-1-7361515-7-0

Dedication

To my loving husband, Scott, my biggest cheerleader.
I love walking this God journey with you!

Acknowledgements

Great thanks to the founder of Missio Global
J. Lee Simmons. You have been an amazing mentor.
Thank you for believing in us.

Thanks to Judah Davis and Jack Henry for their input and
editing of this book.

The Cross Series

The Cross book series is for Christian spiritual growth focusing on foundational discipleship. The material is best used in a one-on-one discipleship relationship or in micro-groups of up to four people. The Cross Series is designed as a growth track that leads to the church-based Missio Global School of Ministry. It can also be used as valuable equipping material for general Christian discipleship.

CrossWalk - Vital Steps in Your Walk with God

Vital steps for Christ-followers who want to deepen their walk with God. *CrossWalk* is foundational discipleship.

CrossFire - A New Way of Living (Books 1 and 2)

Transforming personal values to ones that follow biblical principles, which results in a powerful new way of living!

This material is free upon request in pdf format for use outside the United States. It can be reproduced for training purposes only.

Missio Global School of Ministry

This material is used in conjunction with the Missio Global School of Ministry, a partnership between Missio Global and churches around the world. The School is a valuable one or three-year training program that is based in the local church. It is a proven tool that churches can use to equip their congregation and develop emerging leaders.

For information on hosting a School of Ministry in your church, contact us at: team@missioglobal.org or see missioglobal.org.

Table of Contents

Preface

My husband and I have been missionaries for many years, so travel has become an accepted part of our lives. We have traveled by plane, car, bus, and train in the United States and abroad. We have experienced late arrivals, canceled flights, flat tires, and even had a car stolen. We have had to cancel or delay a trip, but we have never failed to arrive home.

Walking with God is a journey. Sometimes we may be delayed, arrive late, or even have to cancel plans, but God's goal is for us to make it home to him. Hebrews 12:1 says, "Therefore, since we are surrounded by so great a cloud of witnesses, let us also lay aside every weight, and sin which clings so closely, and let us run with endurance the race that is set before us."

Our goal is to help each follower of Christ to start well to better insure they finish well. There may be rough roads along the way, but with Jesus by your side you will reach your destination. Your journey to fulfill your calling as God's child is completed by taking many steps. Make the most of the ones presented here. It is our prayer that this book helps you on this wonderful journey of following Jesus, or enables you to guide someone else on their journey.

Sherri L. Dalton
January 2021

How to Use *CrossWalk*

This book is a great tool to disciple a Christian to a deeper walk with Christ and develop a firm foundation in the Kingdom of God. The book can be used to disciple new Christians as well as established believers. The information in this book helps the believer to develop a deeper relationship with God, introduces the Kingdom of God, and facilitates the connection to a community of believers (the church).

This material can be used to disciple a single person or a small group of Christians (preferably six or less people) on what it means to be a disciple by providing a foundation of knowledge on God, the Kingdom of God, and the Bible, plus weekly activities. The material is presented in an easy-to-follow study format that includes reading Bible passages and capturing the meaning in the scriptures.

The book is organized in lessons or "steps" that will be completed over a period of 8 weeks. Each week moves the person from where they are now to greater spiritual maturity as they gain a greater understanding of the Bible and develop a stronger walk with God. The goal is to become a mature disciple of God.

Each lesson includes the following items:

First Thoughts: Provides an explanation of the topic and begins to set expectations for the disciple-in-training to consider and think about for the week, setting the framework for the Bible study.

A Look at the Word: A series of Bible passages followed by questions to reinforce the topic. Over the course of the training the following books of the Bible will be read—Gospel of John, 1 John, Ephesians, and Colossians.

Application: Exercises for reflection and application of the truths examined in the Bible study for each week.

Next Steps: Provides "homework" for each lesson that reinforces what was learned that week, including:

Bible Reading This Week – Specific Bible readings that will also be included in the discussions during the meetings.

Memorize – A key Bible verse is provided to memorize in order to solidify God's purpose and/or promise.

Prayer – Provides a guideline for praying each week, talking with God like you would a close friend.

Share The Good News – Identify others to pray for during the week and share your faith story.

Recommendations for Discipleship:

Prior to the first meeting:

- The leader should read the entire book and become familiar with the different steps, answer the questions, and practice the "Next Steps."
- Schedule and meet weekly for about an hour.
- As much as possible everyone should read each step before the meeting and answer the questions.
- During the meeting you can review the Application and Next Steps to be completed before the next meeting.
- Follow the different sections of each step and allow each person to share their thoughts and experiences on each section.
- Share examples from your own journey. Make the meeting personal. Be vulnerable, sharing your weaknesses as well as your strengths.
- Share from your heart what God is teaching you through this journey.
- The leader should pray regularly for the disciple-in-training or the participants in the small group throughout the weeks they are meeting together.

Introduction

We are so glad you made the commitment to complete *CrossWalk!* It will provide a great boost in your growth in God. It is best to read the book with an experienced disciple of Jesus because your relationship with God is always meant to be lived in community with other believers. As you study this book you will grow to the extent that you engage in the spiritual disciplines presented.

As you move forward on your journey, surround yourself with people who can help you grow in your knowledge of and love for God. The best way to do this is to be a member of a good Christian, Bible-believing *local church* that stands firm on the truths of the Bible. This will help you grow spiritually as you "put on the new self, created to be like God in true righteousness and holiness" (Ephesians 4:24). Walking with Jesus is about moving from your old ways of thinking and behavior to developing new attitudes and behaviors that glorify God. God never intended you to walk alone, but to journey with other like-minded disciples of Christ through the local church.

Another important step that will move you forward in your walk with God is *water baptism*. Water Baptism does not save you, but comes after salvation as a public declaration of putting your faith in a crucified, buried, and risen Savior. Just as Jesus died, was buried, and then resurrected, water baptism symbolizes your death to sin, the burial of your old life (as you are submerged under water), and your resurrection to a new life in Christ (as you are raised up out of the water). For this reason, water baptism, as seen in the Bible, was always done by immersion (being covered over with water). Speak with someone in your church about being baptized. They may have a class or an orientation that you must complete first. Be sure to find out what requirements are necessary for you to take this very important step in your walk with Jesus. Romans 6:3-5 and

Colossians 2:11-12 are good references to learn more about baptism.

Enjoy this journey of a lifetime with Jesus and with his church. Following Jesus means you have been set free from the power of sin, shame, and death, and you are made alive to God. Jesus promises to never leave you, and he has given you his Holy Spirit to live inside you, correct you, give you understanding, and guide you on your journey. Through good or difficult times, you will never regret trusting Jesus as your lifelong companion!

Step 1

Walking with God
Understanding Salvation

FIRST THOUGHTS

Turning your life over to God and walking with him is the most important decision of your life! When we admit our sins separate us from God and receive Jesus as the Son of God who died for our sins, we are saved from the penalty of sin, which is death and eternal separation from God. God calls this salvation. We have crossed over from being a sinner to being a child of God, and our journey of walking with God begins! We deserved death because of our sin, but Jesus took the penalty in our place when he died on the cross and was resurrected. When we receive this gift of salvation, God not only calls us his child, but he also gives us eternal life. He wants us to be with him forever!

When we confess Jesus as our Lord, we receive eternal life. After we die physically, our spirit lives on forever with God in heaven. But what happens now in this present life? What does it mean to live a life dedicated to Christ in God's kingdom now on earth? Is it simply going to church, reading the Bible, or being a good person? The word Christian literally means "Christ follower." God wants us to grow in our knowledge of who he is and what is right, through reading the Bible, prayer, and discipleship. He wants us to grow in relationship with other believers by participating in a local church, our new spiritual family. And he wants us to understand the privileges and authority which are available through our access to God's kingdom here and now.

Receiving salvation and being a Christian is not just about doing good deeds, following rules and regulations, or performing rituals. The only way to receive salvation and have eternal life is to put your faith in Jesus who died for your sins, taking the penalty you deserve. Living a life dedicated to Christ means obeying his teachings as found in the Bible. Going to church, reading the Bible, and obeying God are a *result* of following Jesus and living in relationship to him.

A LOOK AT THE WORD

1. Mark 1:14-15 – *Now after John was put in prison, Jesus went into Galilee, proclaiming the good news of God. 15 "The time has come," he said. "The kingdom of God has come near. Repent and believe the good news!"* (NIV)

   • What did Jesus tell people to do?

   The word "repent" does not simply mean "stop sinning." It actually means "to change your way of thinking." Therefore, another way to say this verse is: "Jesus went into Galilee, proclaiming the good news of God, and saying, 'The time has finally come! Because the kingdom of God is within reach, *change your purpose, think differently*, and believe the good news.'"

2. 1 John 5:11-13 – *And this is the testimony, that God gave us eternal life, and this life is in his Son. 12 Whoever has the Son has life; whoever does not have the Son of God does not have life. 13 I write these things to you who believe in the name of the Son of God, that you may know that you have eternal life.*

   • Who gives us eternal life?

- Where is this life found?

- Who has eternal life?

- Who does not have eternal life?

- This was written to you who believe in the name of the Son of God so that you may _____ that you have eternal life.

- How can you clearly know that you have eternal life?

3. Romans 3:23 – *For all have sinned and fall short of the glory of God.*
   - God is perfect and full of glory. Is anyone sinless and perfect like God?

4. Romans 6:23 – *For the wages of sin is death, but the free gift of God is eternal life in Christ Jesus our Lord.*
   - What is the wage we receive for sin?

   - What is the free gift of God and through whom?

5. Romans 10:9-10 – *...because, if you confess with your mouth that Jesus is Lord and believe in your heart that God raised him from the dead, you will be saved. [10]For with the heart one believes and is justified, and with the mouth one confesses and is saved.*
   - What two things do you need to do to be saved?

- Why do you think both are important?

6. Ephesians 2:8-9 – *For by grace you have been saved through faith. And this is not your own doing; it is the gift of God, [9]not a result of works, so that no one may boast.*

   - Through faith you are saved by_____.

   - Who did this, God or you?

   - Grace means favor from God that is undeserving. In other words, it is not the result of your good works. Why?

7. 1 John 3:9 – *No one born of God makes a practice of sinning, for God's seed abides in him; and he cannot keep on sinning, because he has been born of God.*

   - Who does not make a practice of sinning? Why?

APPLICATION

As these verses explain, we are saved when we believe in Jesus Christ through faith, repent of our sins, and confess Jesus as our Lord. Repentance means to think differently, to reconsider, or to change direction. Repenting of our sins allows us to see things differently and as a result, to do things differently. The Bible explains what are the right things to do. We are learners and followers of Jesus. As human beings we will sin again. In fact, the rest of our lives we continue to learn what is sinful and what is not. But as children of God we are given a new heart and we do not pursue sin because we love God.

When we do sin, he calls us to repent (think differently), receive his forgiveness, and continue to follow him. It is important to understand that the strength to change our lives comes from God. Salvation is not something we can earn through good works but is from trusting in Jesus. We do good works because we love Jesus. We can know without a doubt that we are saved because we have God living in our heart and teaching us how to live! Good works are a sign that we are a "new person"—the result of salvation—and that God lives in our heart!

Yes, I know that I am saved and have eternal life. _____

No, I am not sure that I am saved and have eternal life. _____

Write/discuss the difference between feeling sorry for your sins and repenting of your sins.

NEXT STEPS

Bible reading this week

John 1-5. Begin to read the Gospel of John. Try to read one chapter a day for five days each week. John has 21 chapters so you will finish the book in a month. As you read, consider the following questions and discuss them in your next meeting:

- What stood out to me as I read?
- Is there anything I did not understand and need to ask about it?
- Is there anything I need to do in obedience to this text?

Memorize

Romans 6:23 – "For the wages of sin is death, but the free gift of God is eternal life in Christ Jesus our Lord."

Prayer

Pray for 5 minutes a day this week. Simply talk to God like you would a close friend. Thank him for your new life, ask him to lead you through the day, pray for your needs, and ask him to bless the people you are close to. You will learn more about prayer in Step 5.

Step 2

Walking with Jesus
Understanding the Good News

FIRST THOUGHTS

Jesus is the eternal Son of God who existed as God before creation. He and God the Father and the Holy Spirit exist eternally together as Lord. Together they are one God with three distinct persons. We call this the Trinity or the Holy Trinity.

God promised the Jewish nation a Messiah, a king that would save them and reign forever. He also promised to send a blessing to the rest of the world to open a way for their salvation. Jesus is the Messiah (anointed one) who God sent to save the world from sin, death, and eternal punishment. (The word *Christ* is the Greek word used in the New Testament that means "anointed one.") Jesus means "God rescues" or "God saves."

Jesus rescued the world by providing a way for us to reestablish a relationship with God. Jesus' death and resurrection removed the barrier between us and God that our sin had created. As we learned in Step 1, Jesus said the good news is that the kingdom of God is now near (Mark 1:15). In other words, through Jesus we once again have access to God and his kingdom right now! This includes salvation, of course, but salvation is just the doorway into a new life in the kingdom of God. All that we need is found in the kingdom of God, including salvation, righteousness, healing, provision, purpose, freedom, joy, peace, etc! That is good news!

Jesus came the first time as a servant and savior. He set us free from sin and gave us eternal life. He now sits as king at the right hand of God, having all authority in heaven and on earth. Jesus has also given spiritual authority on earth to those who follow him, and that includes you! He will empower you to live a life of victory and you can help other people do the same. The good news is through Jesus we can overcome the curse of sin and the world system now, experience the life that God created us to live, and then spend eternity with him.

Jesus rules in heaven now, but one day he will return to rule on earth. It is important to know what the New Testament tells us about Jesus as the divine, eternal son of God—He is both the Son of God and God the Son.

A LOOK AT THE WORD

1. Colossians 1:15-22 – *He is the image of the invisible God, the firstborn of all creation.* [16]*For by him all things were created, in heaven and on earth, visible and invisible, whether thrones or dominions or rulers or authorities – all things were created through him and for him.* [17]*And he is before all things, and in him all things hold together.* [18]*And he is the head of the body, the church. He is the beginning, the firstborn from the dead, that in everything he might be preeminent.* [19]*For in him all the fullness of God was pleased to dwell,* [20]*and through him to reconcile to himself all things, whether on earth or in heaven, making peace by the blood of his cross.* [21]*And you, who once were alienated and hostile in mind, doing evil deeds,* [22]*he has now reconciled in his body of flesh by his death, in order to present you holy and blameless and above reproach before him.*

- According to verses 15, 17, and 18 who is Jesus?

- What was created by him (verse 16)?

- What dwells in Jesus (verse 19)?

- What was done through Jesus (verse 20)?

- Before knowing Jesus, who were we and what did we do (verse 21)?

- Jesus reconciled us in his body of flesh by his death to do what? (verse 22)

According to this passage in Colossians 1, Jesus is God. Jesus reconciled, through his death, those who were hostile and doing evil deeds to present them holy (perfect in every way), blameless (no longer held accountable for any sin), and above reproach (nothing to criticize) before God.

- How does it make you feel to know that God now sees you as holy, blameless and above reproach?

2. Philippians 2:3-11 – *Do nothing out of selfish ambition or vain conceit. Rather in humility value others above yourselves, ⁴ not looking to your own interests but each of you to the interests of others. ⁵ In your relationships with one another, have the same mindset as Christ Jesus: ⁶Who, being in very nature God, did not consider equality with God something to be used to his own advantage (to hold onto);⁷rather, he made himself nothing by taking the very nature of a servant, being made in human likeness. ⁸And*

being found in appearance as a man, he humbled himself by becoming obedient to death—even death on a cross! ⁹Therefore God exalted him to the highest place and gave him the name that is above every name, ¹⁰that at the name of Jesus every knee should bow, in heaven and on earth and under the earth, ¹¹and every tongue acknowledge (confess) that Jesus Christ is Lord, to the glory of God the Father. (NIV) (parenthesis added)

- If you walk in humility, what will you do for others (verses 3-4)?

- How did Jesus show his humility (verses 6-8)?

- As a result of Jesus' humility, what did God do for him (verses 9-11).

APPLICATION

As we discovered in the first step last week, we are to learn to think differently as we follow Jesus. God wants us to consider others as more significant (important) than ourselves and look to the interest of others as well as our own interests. Having this attitude of humility will help us to think like Jesus, who set aside his heavenly existence to live as a human being with all its limitations. Then he went even further, becoming obedient to the point of death on a humiliating cross. Because of his humility and obedience, God exalted him to the highest place. Jesus promised that those who humble themselves will be exalted (Matthew 23:12). We can trust God with our reputation as Jesus did.

What are some areas where you can humble yourself, considering others as more significant?

NEXT STEPS

Bible reading this week

John 6-10. Continue to read the Gospel of John, reading one chapter a day for five days each week. As you read, consider the following questions and discuss them in your next meeting:
- What stood out to me as I read?
- Is there anything I did not understand and need to ask about it?
- Is there anything I need to do in obedience to this text?

Memorize

Philippians 2:9 – "Therefore God exalted him (Jesus) to the highest place and gave him the name that is above every name."

Prayer

Pray for 5 minutes a day this week. Simply talk to God like you would a close friend. Thank him for your new life, ask him to lead you through the day, pray for your needs, and ask him to bless the people you are close to. You will learn more about prayer in Step 4 5.

If you could have one prayer request answered, guaranteed, what would it be? Write it below. When it is answered, come back and write that date and share your testimony with your discipler.

Date: _____   Prayer Request:

Step 3

Walking as an Ambassador
Sharing the Good News

FIRST THOUGHTS

The good news of salvation and access to the kingdom of God is indeed the greatest news on earth! Just as you received this life-giving message, you can share it with others. In fact, followers of Jesus are called to be "ambassadors" for God here on earth. An ambassador is someone authorized to speak on behalf of a higher authority, like a king or president. (You can read about this in your Bible at 2 Corinthians 5:16-21.)

Believe it or not, God is calling you to be his ambassador and present his message of good news to your family and friends (and even to those you have yet to meet). You don't need to have all the answers or know what the Bible says about all of life's issues. You don't have to wait until your life is all in order. Just share **your** story of what God has done for you! Share the simple message about God's love and forgiveness for those who turn to Jesus and that a new life awaits all who do!

There was a man in the Bible whose life was a total mess, a hell on earth! He lived in tombs and cut himself with stones. He even broke off chains from his hands and feet; no one was strong enough to subdue him. But one day Jesus arrived and cast out multiple demons from this man and he became whole and in his right mind. He wanted to go with Jesus, but Jesus told him instead to, "Go home to your own people and tell them how much the Lord has done for you, and how he has had mercy on you" (Mark 5:19). That is Jesus' call to you as well. Go and tell others all that the Lord has done for you, and how he has been merciful to you.

A LOOK AT THE WORD

1. 2 Corinthians 5:18-21 – *All this is from God, who reconciled us to himself through Christ and gave us the ministry of reconciliation: [19]that God was reconciling the world to himself in Christ, not counting people's sins against them. And he has committed to us the message of reconciliation. [20]We are therefore Christ's ambassadors, as though God were making his appeal through us. We implore you on Christ's behalf: Be reconciled to God. [21]God made him who had no sin to be sin for us, so that in him we might become the righteousness of God.* (NIV)

   - What is the ministry we have from God (verse 18)?

   - How did God reconcile the world to himself (verse 19)? What does that mean?

   - How does God tell people to be reconciled to himself (verse 20)? What is the title of the person who represents God in this way (verse 20)?

2. Mark 5:18-20 (full story is Mark 5:1-20) – *As Jesus was getting into the boat, the man who had been demon-possessed begged to go with him. [19]Jesus did not let him, but said, "Go home to your own people and tell them how much the Lord has done for you, and how he has had mercy on you." [20]So the man went away and began to tell in the*

Decapolis how much Jesus had done for him. And all the people were amazed. (NIV)

- When Jesus called his disciples he told them "follow me." When the man who had been demon-possessed wanted to follow Jesus, what did he tell him to do? What was the result of his obedience?

3. Mark 16:15 (full context is Mark16:15-20) – *He said to them, "Go into all the world and preach the gospel (good news) to all creation."* (NIV) (parenthesis added)

- Before the resurrected Jesus ascended into heaven, what command did he give to his followers? Why?

- How can you obey this command?

APPLICATION

Every disciple of Christ has a story he can tell about how God reached out to him and made his presence known. In the church, this is sometimes called a "testimony," but it is simply your personal story about giving your life to Christ. As you share your story with others, it helps to actually first write it down so that you can organize your thoughts. Take time this week to write down your story. Be careful to make it short. You should be able to say it in about 90 seconds! You can practice sharing it with your discipler. Write your story in three paragraphs following this pattern:

- What was your life like before knowing Jesus?
- What happened in your life for you to accept Jesus as your Lord?
- How has God changed your life?

When you share about your own salvation you can utilize some of the Bible verses that you studied in the A LOOK AT THE WORD section in **Step 1**: Walking with God – Understanding Salvation. The verses of Romans 3:23, Romans 6:23, and Romans 10:9-10 are especially helpful in explaining salvation, including how someone can receive Jesus as their Savior and Lord.

Another simple way to think about and explain salvation through Jesus is called the ABC's of salvation. You can remember it like this:

A – **Admit** that you are a sinner and that your sins are what have separated you from God.

B – **Believe** in your heart that Jesus' death on the cross and resurrection paid the penalty for your sins that you cannot pay, and that faith in Jesus is the only way you can enter a relationship with God.

C – **Confess** with your mouth that Jesus is your Lord, turn from your own way of living, and follow Jesus and his ways.

As a second application, write down the names of three people that you will pray for daily to come to Jesus just like you did. Lay your hands on your written story and pray for opportunities to share it with one of the people you listed (or anyone else God may bring). Read your story over and over until you can say it without needing to read it.

NEXT STEPS

Bible reading this week

John 11-15. Continue to read the Gospel of John, reading one chapter a day for five days each week. As you read, consider the following questions and discuss them in your next meeting:

- What stood out to me as I read?
- Is there anything I did not understand and need to ask about it?
- Is there anything I need to do in obedience to this text?

Memorize

2 Corinthians 5:20 – We are therefore Christ's ambassadors, as though God were making his appeal through us. We implore you on Christ's behalf: Be reconciled to God.

Prayer

Pray for 5 minutes a day this week. Simply talk to God like you would a close friend. Thank him for your new life, ask him to lead you through the day, pray for your needs, and ask him to bless the people you are close to. You will learn more about prayer in Step 4 5.

Share the Good News

Write out your story this week and read it three times a day so that you are comfortable sharing it without reading it.

Make a list of three people you will pray for to come to know Jesus. Pray for an opportunity to share your story about knowing Jesus with them.

Step 4

Walking in the Word
Knowing God through the Bible

FIRST THOUGHTS

God calls his messages to us his "word." One of the best ways to know God and how he expects us to live in this world is by reading his word, the Bible. How do we know what God is like? The Bible tells us that God is holy, righteous, loving, merciful, and many other things. God wants us to be like him. In the Bible we learn who he is and how he desires us to live in relationship with him and one another.

Here is some basic background information on the Bible:

- **The Bible is a collection of God's messages to his people**, given to his servants, who wrote God's messages down and passed them on to all generations.

- **There are 66 books in the Bible**, 39 in the Old Testament and 27 in the New Testament.

- The **Old Testament** was originally written in Hebrew and Aramaic; the **New Testament** was originally written in Greek.

- **The Bible was written under the inspiration of the Holy Spirit over a period of about 2,000 years** (the oldest book, Job, was written close to 4,000 years ago) by over 40 different authors from many different backgrounds—from shepherds, farmers, tent-makers, and fishermen, to educated physicians, priests, philosophers, and kings.

- **Despite the many years it took to write the Bible** and the varied background of its authors and their cultures, it is an incredibly cohesive and unified book.

The Bible contains as many as 7,000 promises to God's followers! It is not only our source to know God better, but we can study and declare scriptures to cultivate our faith to receive God's promises and use it as a weapon in spiritual battles. As we pray according to God's word, we bring God's kingdom and will into whatever situation we encounter here on earth, as Jesus instructed us to do in Matthew 6:10 (The Lord's Prayer).

A LOOK AT THE WORD

1. Hebrews 4:12 – *For the word of God is living and active, sharper than any two-edged sword, piercing to the division of soul and of spirit, of joints and of marrow, and discerning the thoughts and intentions of the heart.*

   - What are the first two words that describe the word of God?

   - It is sharper than a sword. What does a sword do? What does the word of God do?

This verse is a graphic explanation of how God's word can distinguish between the godly and ungodly, good and evil, even within our own minds and hearts. It is a powerful tool to determine what is godly and ungodly in our society, but it also can penetrate into our inner being and reveal our own sins like wrong motives, lustful thoughts, and selfishness.

2. Psalm 119:105 – *Your word is a lamp to my feet, a light to my path.*

    • When you are walking along a dark path, what will a lamp do for you? How can God's word do that for you?

3. Psalm 119:130 – *The unfolding of your words gives light; it imparts understanding to the simple.*

    • What effect does the word of God have on us?

4. Psalm 119:133 – *Keep steady my steps according to your promise (word), and let no iniquity (sin) get dominion over me.* (parentheses added)

    • What will happen in our life when we follow God's word?

5. Psalm 119:160 – *The sum of your word is truth, and every one of your righteous rules endures forever.*

    • What words are used to describe God's word? What does that mean to you?

6. Isaiah 40:8 – *The grass withers, the flowers fall, but the word of our God will stand forever.*

    • What happens to earthly things like grass and flowers? What is God's word like? How does that make you feel?

7. Isaiah 55:10-11 – *For as the rain and the snow come down from heaven and do not return there but water the earth, making it bring forth and sprout, giving seed to the sower and bread to the eater, ¹¹so shall be my word that goes out from my mouth; it shall not return to me empty, but it shall accomplish that which I purpose, and shall succeed in the thing for which I sent it.*

   • What does the word of God do?

8. Matthew 4:4 – *But he (Jesus) answered, "It is written: 'Man shall not live by bread alone, but by every word that comes from the mouth of God.'"* (parentheses added)

   • Our lives should be sustained not just by food but by what else?

9. Luke 11:28 – *But he (Jesus) said, "Blessed rather are those who hear the word of God and keep (obey) it."* (parentheses added)

   • According to this verse, what two things must someone do to be blessed?

APPLICATION

According to the verses this week, reading the Bible reveals the thoughts and intentions of our heart (Heb. 4:12); it lights our path (Ps. 119:105); it gives understanding (Ps. 119:130); its keeps sin from having dominion over us (Ps. 119:133); it endures forever (Ps. 119:160 and Isaiah 40:8); it will accomplish what God sends it forth to do (Is. 55:11); it sustains us like food (Matt. 4:4); and it blesses those who hear and obey it (Luke 11:28).

What verse impacted you the most? How will you apply the truths in your life this coming week? (Write below.)

Are there any Bible promises you can pray for yourself or others? Are there any steps of faith *you* need to take?

NEXT STEPS

Bible reading this week

John 16-21. Read **six chapters** in the Gospel of John this week to finish the book. As you read, consider the following questions and discuss them in your next meeting:

- What stood out to me as I read?
- Is there anything I did not understand and need to ask about it?
- Is there anything I need to do in obedience to this text?

On the weekend, read Psalm 146. According to this psalm, what does God do for those who trust in Him?

Memorize

Psalm 119:105 – Your word is a lamp to my feet, a light to my path.

Prayer

Pray for 5 minutes a day this week. Simply talk to God like you would a close friend. Thank him for your new life, ask him to lead you through the day, pray for your needs, and ask him to bless the people you are close to. You will learn more about prayer in Step 5.

Share the Good News

Continue to practice sharing your story.

Continue to pray for the three people you listed last week to come to know Jesus. Pray for an opportunity to share your story about knowing Jesus with them.

Step 5

Walking in Prayer
Talking and Listening to God

FIRST THOUGHTS

God wants us to know him! We can know God through reading the scriptures but we can also know him through prayer. Prayer is simply a conversation with God. We can talk to him like we talk to a good friend, sharing our pain, joy, desires, and needs. Walking with God is a living, close relationship with him. We should not only talk to him; we also need *to listen* to him.

Just as we must discipline ourselves to listen to people, we need to discipline ourselves to listen to God. God speaks to people in different ways, depending on their personality, gifts, and life experiences. But we can be assured that God wants to listen and speak to us. Many times he uses the Bible to speak to us. And we can also use the Bible to speak to God. He wants to make us like his son, Jesus, and this only happens when we are close to him in prayer and Bible reading, trusting and obeying him throughout our days.

A LOOK AT THE WORD

1. Exodus 33:11a – *Thus the Lord used to speak to Moses face to face, as a man speaks to his friend.*

   • How did God speak to Moses?

2. Psalm 66:17-20 – *I cried to him with my mouth, and high praise was on my tongue.* ¹⁸*If I had cherished iniquity (sin)*

in my heart, the Lord would not have listened. [19]But truly God has listened; he has attended to the voice of my prayer. [20]Blessed be God, because he has not rejected my prayer or removed his steadfast love from me!

- What does God do for the person who does not cherish sin in their heart?

3. Psalm 102:17 – *He regards the prayer of the destitute; he does not despise their prayer.*

- What does God do for the destitute?"

4. Proverbs 15:8 – *The sacrifice of the wicked is an abomination to the Lord, but the prayer of the upright is acceptable to him.*

- Whose prayer does God accept?

5. Matthew 21:22 – *And whatever you ask in prayer, you will receive, if you have faith.*

- What happens when we ask in faith?

6. Philippians 4:6 – *Do not be anxious about anything, but in everything by prayer and supplication with thanksgiving let your requests be made known to God.*

- What are we to do instead of being anxious?

7. Colossians 4:2 – *Continue steadfastly in prayer, being watchful in it with thanksgiving.*

- How can you continue steadfastly in prayer?

8. James 5:13-16 – *Is anyone among you suffering? Let him pray. Is anyone cheerful? Let him sing praise. [14]Is anyone among you sick? Let him call the elders of the church, and let them pray over him, anointing him with oil in the name of the Lord. [15]And the prayer of faith will save the one who is sick, and the Lord will raise him up. And if he has committed sins, he will be forgiven. [16]Therefore, confess your sins to one another, and pray for one another, that you may be healed. The prayer of a righteous person has great power as it is working.*

   • When are we to pray for ourselves or others? Why?

9. Acts 10:30-31 – *And Cornelius said: "Four days ago, about this hour, I was praying in my house, at the ninth hour (3:00 pm), and behold, a man stood before me in bright clothing [31]and said, 'Cornelius, your prayer has been heard and your alms have been remembered before God.'"* (parentheses added)

   • Who heard Cornelius' prayer and remembered his alms to the poor?

APPLICATION

A Listening Exercise (10-15 minutes): On the following page, fill in the date next to the sentence "Jesus, this is why I love you so much." Then, take a moment to share with Jesus, in writing, why you love him. Next, close your eyes and quiet your heart and mind before God. Picture yourself as an eight-year-old child and listen to what he says in response. With a childlike faith, fix your mind on Jesus and write a short paragraph of spontaneous flowing thoughts of what you hear God saying to you. (Leave a line space in between your written thoughts and what God speaks to you in response.) If there is time, do this exercise during your time together. Take a few minutes and do it separately using the space below. Discuss what you heard God say to each of you. End your time in prayer. Be sure to do this exercise at least once during the week.

Date: _____

"Jesus, this is why I love you so much."

NEXT STEPS

Bible reading this week

1 John. If you have been reading a chapter a day for five days a week in the Bible, you should have finished the Gospel of John by now. If you did not finish the Gospel of John, complete it this week. If you have finished John, read the short book of 1 John this week. 1 John is a letter written by the apostle John. It is near the very end of the New Testament. As you read, consider the following questions and discuss them in your next meeting:

- What stood out to me as I read?
- Is there anything I did not understand and need to ask about it?
- Is there anything I need to do in obedience to this text?

Memorize

Matthew 21:22 – And whatever you ask in prayer, you will receive, if you have faith.

Prayer

Pray for 5-10 minutes a day this week.

Take a day this week and pray for 20 minutes. Use the ACTS acronym as a guide:

Adoration – Worship God for who he is: Creator, Almighty, Holy God, Savior, Redeemer, Father, Friend, etc. After you worship, take time to be quiet and listen.

Confession – Confess any sins and forgive anyone who may have sinned against you.

Thanksgiving – Thank God for His protection and provision in your life and in the world.

Supplication – Pray for your needs and the needs of others.

Share the Good News

Have you had a chance to share your story? Talk about it with your discipler.

Continue to pray for the three people you listed to come to know Jesus. Pray for an opportunity to share your story about knowing Jesus with them.

Step 6

Walking with the Holy Spirit
Knowing the Power of God

FIRST THOUGHTS

The Holy Spirit is God, not lower than God the Father or God the Son (Jesus), but equal to them in nature and attributes. Because the Holy Spirit is God, he is omnipresent (present everywhere – Ps. 139:7-12), omniscient (knows everything – 1 Cor. 2:9-10), omnipotent (all powerful – Rev. 1:8; Ps. 104:30) and eternal (Deut. 33:27; Heb. 9:14). Like Jesus and the Father, we can have a relationship with the Holy Spirit; we can pray to him just like we can pray to the Father and Jesus.

The Holy Spirit is a person not a power or a force, and his presence is with us now and always. It is the Holy Spirit who comes to live within us when we repent and accept the blood of Jesus as payment for our sins. Jesus told the disciples to wait in Jerusalem until they were baptized with the Holy Spirit (Acts 1:4-5).

In Acts 2:1-4, one hundred and twenty disciples were praying together in Jerusalem and they were all filled with the Holy Spirit. Many of these same disciples were filled again in Acts 4:31. We are to be constantly asking God that we be filled with the Holy Spirit! Someone asked the great American evangelist of the 19th century D. L. Moody, "Why do we need new fillings of the Holy Spirit?" His reply, "Because we leak."

A LOOK AT THE WORD

1. **The Holy Spirit gives life.**

    Psalm 104:29-30 – *When you hide your face, they are dismayed; when you take away their breath, they die and return to their dust. [30]When you send forth your Spirit, they are created, and you renew the face of the ground.*

    *   What happens when God sends forth His Spirit?

2. **The Holy Spirit sets us free.**

    Romans 8:1-2 – *There is therefore now no condemnation for those who are in Christ Jesus. [2]For the law of the Spirit of life has set you free in Christ Jesus from the law of sin and death.*

    *   From what does the Holy Spirit set us free?

3. **The Holy Spirit gives power for service.**

    Acts 1:8 – *But you will receive power when the Holy Spirit has come upon you, and you will be my witnesses in Jerusalem and in all Judea and Samaria and to the end of the earth.*

    *   For what service does the Holy Spirit give power?

4. **The Holy Spirit is a worker of miracles and gives spiritual gifts.**

    Matthew 12:28 – *But if it is by the Spirit of God that I cast out demons, then the kingdom of God has come upon you.*

    *   How did Jesus cast out demons?

1 Corinthians 12:8-11 – *For to one is given through the Spirit the utterance (word) of wisdom, and to another the utterance (word) of knowledge according to the same Spirit, ⁹to another faith by the same Spirit, to another gifts of healing by the one Spirit, ¹⁰to another the working of miracles, to another prophecy, to another the ability to distinguish between spirits, to another various kinds of tongues, to another the interpretation of tongues. ¹¹All these are empowered by one and the same Spirit, who apportions to each one individually as he wills.*

- List the kinds of gifts we can receive through the Holy Spirit:

5. The Holy Spirit directs and guides God's people.

Galatians 5:16, 22-23 – *¹⁶But I say, walk by the Spirit, and you will not gratify the desires of the flesh...²²But the fruit of the Spirit is love, joy, peace, patience, kindness, goodness, faithfulness, ²³gentleness, self-control; against such things there is no law.*

- What happens when you walk by the Spirit? What is produced?

Romans 8:5, 14 – *⁵Those who live according to the flesh have their minds set on what the flesh desires; but those who live in accordance with the Spirit have their minds set on what Spirit desires...¹⁴For those who are led by the Spirit of God are children of God.* (NIV)

- How does God refer to those who are led by the Spirit?

6. The Holy Spirit purifies.

1 Corinthians 6:11 – *But you were washed, you were sanctified, you were justified in the name of the Lord Jesus Christ and by the Spirit of our God.*

- We were purified in the name of the Lord Jesus Christ by whom?

7. The Holy Spirit brings revelation.

2 Peter 1:20-21 – *...knowing this first of all, that no prophecy of Scripture comes from someone's own interpretation. ²¹For no prophecy was ever produced by the will of man, but men spoke from God as they were carried along by the Holy Spirit.*

- How did men write Scripture (the Bible)?

8. The Holy Spirit displays God's kingdom.

Romans 14:17 – *For the kingdom of God is not a matter of eating and drinking but of righteousness and peace and joy in the Holy Spirit.*

- How does the Holy Spirit display God's kingdom?

9. The Holy Spirit lives in us.

1 John 4:13 – *This is how we know that we live in him and he in us: He has given us of his Spirit.* (NIV)

- How do we know that we live with God and he is with us now?

10. The Holy Spirit gives understanding.

John 14:26 – *But the Helper, the Holy Spirit, whom the Father will send in my name, he will teach you all things and bring to your remembrance all that I have said to you.*

John 16:13 – *When the Spirit of truth comes, he will guide you into all the truth, for he will not speak on his own authority, but whatever he hears he will speak, and he will declare to you the things that are to come.*

- How will the Holy Spirit give us understanding?

11. The Holy Spirit brings unity.

Ephesians 4:1-3 – *I therefore, a prisoner for the Lord, urge you to walk in a manner worthy of the calling to which you have been called, ²with all humility and gentleness, with patience, bearing with one another in love, ³eager to maintain the unity of the Spirit in the bond of peace.*

- When we walk in humility, gentleness, and patience, bearing with one another in love, what is the result?

12. Negative responses to the Holy Spirit:

Acts 7:51 – *You stiff-necked people, uncircumcised in heart and ears, you always resist the Holy Spirit. As your fathers did, so do you.*

Ephesians 4:30 – *And do not grieve the Holy Spirit of God, by whom you were sealed for the day of redemption.*

1 Thessalonians 5:19 – *Do not quench the Spirit.*

Acts 5:3 – *But Peter said, "Ananias, why has Satan filled your heart to lie to the Holy Spirit and to keep back for yourself part of the proceeds of the land?"*

Luke 12:10 – *And everyone who speaks a word against the Son of Man will be forgiven, but the one who blasphemes against the Holy Spirit will not be forgiven.*

- What are some negative things we can do against the Holy Spirit?

APPLICATION

- Write today's date.
- Write down anything you need from the Holy Spirit (direction, guidance, understanding of scripture, a miracle, healing, provision, unity, purity, etc.)
- Write down scriptures that you can declare to cultivate your faith. (Ask other people if you need help.)
- Ask the Holy Spirit to show you any barriers that may be hindering you from receiving an answer from God (e.g.

anyone you need to forgive or ask to forgive you; any doubt or discouragement, etc.).
- Discuss these with your leader and pray together. When your prayer is answered, come back to this prayer and write the date it was answered.

NEXT STEPS

Bible reading this week

Ephesians 1-6. (If you only read 5 chapters this week you can read chapter 6 next week because the next book you read is only 4 chapters.) As you read, consider the following questions and discuss them in your next meeting:
- What stood out to me as I read?
- Is there anything I did not understand and need to ask about it?
- Is there anything I need to do in obedience to this text?

Memorize

Galatians 5:22-23 – But the fruit of the Spirit is love, joy, peace, patience, kindness, goodness, faithfulness, [23]gentleness, self-control; against such things there is no law.

Prayer

Try to pray every day for 10-15 minutes using the ACTS acronym as a guide:

Adoration – Worship God for who he is: Creator, Almighty, Holy God, Savior, Redeemer, Father, Friend, etc. After you worship, take time to be quiet and listen.

Confession – Confess any sins and forgive anyone who may have sinned against you.

Thanksgiving – Thank God for His protection and provision in your life and in the world.

Supplication – Pray for your needs and the needs of others.

Fast (do not eat) for one meal this week and take that time to pray instead.

Fasting is a spiritual discipline believers combine with prayer. It reveals what controls us and helps us to focus on God. This is helpful especially during times of crisis or when we are urgently needing an answer from God. Jesus promises that when we fast we receive a reward (Matthew 6:18).

Share the Good News

Have you had a chance to share your story? Talk about it with your discipler.

Perhaps you could specifically serve someone in a way that could open the door for you to share the good news with them.

Can you add a name to your prayer list? Continue to pray for the people you listed to come to know Jesus. Pray for an opportunity to share your story about knowing Jesus with them.

Step 7

Walking in Freedom
Fighting from a Place of Victory

FIRST THOUGHTS

There is no greater freedom than living in the fullness of all that God has in his kingdom! The Bible says, "The Lord is the Spirit, and where the Spirit is, there is freedom" (2 Corinthians 3:17). It's not freedom from taking responsibilities or to live however you want, but it's freedom from the penalty and power of sin and death. It is freedom to know Jesus and fulfill the calling of God in your life.

But there are adversaries in this life (the devil and his league of demons) who always seek to kill, steal, and destroy your freedom. While you should remain mindful of the devil's schemes, you must remember that you are NOT fighting *for* the victory; Jesus already won the victory through his death and resurrection. You are fighting *from* a place of victory. You are on the "higher ground!"

The devil has no power that can defeat you when you stand firm in Christ and on his words. The only way the devil can defeat you is to trick you into believing a lie that leads into disobedience. He'll try to convince you that you aren't good enough or that God's word doesn't always "work," among endless other lies. He will try to exploit a point of weakness in your life.

One of the greatest ways to stand firm in your freedom is memorizing Bible verses and declaring them daily. Jesus did exactly this when the devil tried to convince him to reject

God's ways and purpose for his life. The weapon of Jesus against the temptations of the devil was *declaring* (not just knowing) the Word of God. *You need to know and declare the Word of God.*

Start by selecting three verses that you can read repeatedly and memorize. Write the verses down by hand (this will help you memorize them better) and begin your day by declaring the verses out loud. Don't just read them or speak them softly; declare them! They will be a shield and sword for you to walk in the freedom that Christ won for you!

A LOOK AT THE WORD

1. Lies and Strongholds

2 Corinthians 10:3-5 – *³For though we live in the world, we do not wage war as the world does. ⁴The weapons we fight with are not the weapons of the world. On the contrary, they have divine power to demolish strongholds. ⁵We demolish arguments and every pretension that sets itself up against the knowledge of God, and we take captive every thought to make it obedient to Christ.* (NIV)

- How does the world fight?

- How do followers of Jesus fight?

- What is a stronghold (verse 5) and how do we tear it down practically?

2. Deception

Colossians 2:6-8 – *So then, just as you received Christ Jesus as Lord, continue to live your lives in him, [7] rooted and built up in him, strengthened in the faith as you were taught, and overflowing with thankfulness. [8] See to it that no one takes you captive through hollow and deceptive philosophy, which depends on human tradition and the elemental spiritual forces of this world rather than on Christ.* (NIV)

- How are we to live in Christ?

- Why is worldly philosophy hollow and deceptive?

- Jesus is the truth and so is the Bible. What are practical ways can we learn truth and obey it?

3. Temptation

Jesus was tempted by the devil – The Holy Spirit led Jesus into the wilderness where he fasted for 40 days. The devil came and tempted him, first telling him to make the stones into bread. Jesus answered, "It is written: 'Man shall not live on bread alone (Luke 4:4).'" Next, the devil showed him all the kingdoms of the world and said that if Jesus worshipped him he would give him all their splendor and authority. Jesus responded, saying, "It is written: 'Worship the Lord your God and serve him only (Luke 4: 8).'" The third temptation was as follows:

Luke 4:9-14 – *The devil led him to Jerusalem and had him stand on the highest point of the temple. "If you are the Son of God," he said, "throw yourself down from here. [10] For it is written: 'He will command his angels concerning you to guard you carefully; [11] they will lift you up in their hands, so that you will not strike your foot against a stone.'" [12] Jesus answered, "It is said: 'Do not put the Lord your God to the test.'" [13] When the devil had finished all this tempting, he left him until an opportune time. [14] Jesus returned to Galilee in the power of the Spirit, and news about him spread through the whole countryside.* (NIV)

- Satan tempted Jesus the first time, challenging his deity, to meet an immediate need. The second time Satan tempted Jesus he offered him power and riches. What was the third temptation (See also John 8:50 and 54) How did Jesus respond?

- When Jesus said, "It is written" (or "it is said"), what was he quoting?

- Luke 4:1 says, "Jesus, **full** of the Holy Spirit, left the Jordan and was led by the Spirit into the wilderness." How did Jesus leave the wilderness in verse 14?

- Spiritual victory gives us greater power and authority over sin and demons. In what ways can you respond when tempted by sin, people, or demons?

APPLICATION

From the scriptures above it is clear the weapons we fight with are the name of Jesus and the Word of God, the Bible. The more we know Jesus and the Bible, the better equipped we are to win the battle against sin and demons. Ephesians 6:17 says we are to take the "sword of the Spirit, which is the *word* of God." In this passage, in Greek, the "word" is not referring to just what is written in the Bible. It is the word spoken to us by the Holy Spirit. This shows that we need to know the written word of God (the Bible) and also be able to discern the Holy Spirit speaking a "word" to us in a moment of need.

Most of us have a specific sin issue that we battle. The solution is using the word of God to stand firm in freedom and holiness. James 1:21 says, "So get rid of all the filth and evil in your lives, and humbly accept the *word* God has *planted in your hearts*, for it has the *power* to save your souls" (New Living Translation – italics added). Planting the word of God in your heart will help you stay in victory over this issue! The specific sin is a "life" issue and the antidote is a "life" verse. Find a life verse that applies to your situation. Your discipler can help your find one.

Include this verse in the three verses you are to choose this week as described in the "First Thoughts" in this step. Write down the verses and begin to memorize and declare them every day. Choose scriptures that speak faith and victory. Remember, you are fighting and living from a place of victory not defeat! Share the verses with your discipler.

NEXT STEPS

Bible reading this week

Colossians 1-4. Colossians only has 4 chapters so read one chapter a day for four days this week. If you are behind in your reading, you can use other days to catch up. As you read, consider the following questions and discuss them in your next meeting:

- What stood out to me as I read?
- Is there anything I did not understand and need to ask about it?
- Is there anything I need to do in obedience to this text?

Memorize

Ephesians 6:17 – Take the helmet of salvation and the sword of the Spirit, which is the word of God.

Prayer

Try to pray every day for 10-15 minutes using the ACTS acronym as a guide.

Adoration – Worship God for who he is: Creator, Almighty, Holy God, Savior, Redeemer, Father, Friend, etc. After you worship, take time to be quiet and listen.

Confession – Confess any sins and forgive anyone who may have sinned against you.

Thanksgiving – Thank God for His protection and provision in your life and in the world.

Supplication – Pray for your needs and the needs of others.

Share the Good News

Have you had a chance to share your story? Talk about it with your discipler.

Perhaps you could specifically serve someone in a way that could open the door for you to share the good news with them.

Continue to pray for the people you listed to come to know Jesus. Pray for an opportunity to share your story about knowing Jesus with them.

Step 8

Walking with the Church
Knowing God through Community

FIRST THOUGHTS

In a general sense, the church is the community of all true believers, made up of those who are truly saved, for all time.[1] The term "church" may be applied to a small group, a local congregation, or the church around the world. It is not a building, but consists of people who form a church body in relationship with God and with each other. The church is referred to in scripture as a family (1 Tim. 5:1-2; Matt. 12:49-50; 2 Cor. 6:18), the bride of Christ (Eph. 5:32; Rev. 19:7-9), a new temple of living stones (1 Pet. 2:4-8), a holy priesthood (1 Pet. 2:5), the household of God (1Tim. 3:15) and the body of Christ (1 Cor. 12:12-27).

Because the church is the people of God, it is important to spend time with other disciples of Jesus so you can grow and be encouraged in your faith, learn about the importance of baptism and communion, study the Bible with others, pray, confess sins, and grow in spiritual maturity. As the church, we minister to God through worship and obedience to his teachings, we minister to believers by serving and giving our time, talents, and treasure, and we minister to the world through evangelism and mercy.

The Christian church is intended to be a loving fellowship of believers who assemble regularly to engage in various forms of worship, the public reading and teaching of scripture, and corporate prayer. Because the people of God, the church,

---

[1] Wayne Grudem, *Systematic Theology* (Grand Rapids: Zondervan, 2000), p 853.

are a Spirit-led community, use of spiritual gifts is encouraged as long as there is order.

A LOOK AT THE WORD

1. Matthew 16:18 – *And I (Jesus) tell you, you are Peter, and on this rock I will build my church, and the gates of hell shall not prevail against it.* (parentheses added)

    *   Who builds the church?

2. Acts 11:21-26 – *And the hand of the Lord was with them, and a great number who believed turned to the Lord. [22]The report of this came to the ears of the church in Jerusalem, and they sent Barnabas to Antioch. [23]When he came and saw the grace of God, he was glad, and he exhorted them all to remain faithful to the Lord with steadfast purpose, [24]for he was a good man, full of the Holy Spirit and of faith. And a great many people were added to the Lord. [25]So Barnabas went to Tarsus to look for Saul, [26]and when he had found him, he brought him to Antioch. For a whole year they met with the church and taught a great many people. And in Antioch the disciples were first called Christians.*

    *   Who sent Barnabas to Antioch?

    *   Who did Barnabas and Saul teach for a whole year?

3. Acts 12:5 – *So Peter was kept in prison, but earnest prayer for him was made to God by the church.*

    *   Who was praying for Peter when he was in prison?

4. Acts 15:1-4 – *But some men came down from Judea and were teaching the brothers, "Unless you are circumcised according to the custom of Moses, you cannot be saved." ²And after Paul and Barnabas had no small dissension and debate with them, Paul and Barnabas and some of the others were appointed to go up to Jerusalem to the apostles and the elders about this question. ³So, being sent on their way by the church, they passed through both Phoenicia and Samaria, describing in detail the conversion of the Gentiles, and brought great joy to all the brothers. ⁴When they came to Jerusalem, they were welcomed by the church and the apostles and the elders, and they declared all that God had done with them.*

   • Who sent Paul and Barnabas to Jerusalem?

   • Who welcomed Paul and Barnabas in Jerusalem?

5. Ephesians 3:10 – *...so that through the church the manifold (numerous and varied) wisdom of God might now be made known to the rulers and authorities in the heavenly places.* (parentheses added)

   • Who makes known the wisdom of God?

   • Why?

6. 1 Timothy 3:14-15 – *Although I hope to come to you soon, I am writing you these instructions so that, ¹⁵if I am delayed, you will know how people ought to conduct themselves in God's household, which is the church of the living God, the pillar and foundation of the truth.* (NIV)

   • What is the church of the living God?

- What is the purpose of a pillar and a foundation?

- How is the church a pillar and foundation?

7. Ephesians 5:25 – *Husbands, love your wives, as Christ loved the church and gave himself up for her...*
   - What did Christ do for the church to demonstrate his love?

8. Philippians 4:15– *And you Philippians yourselves know that in the beginning of the gospel, when I left Macedonia, no church entered into partnership with me in giving and receiving, except you only.*
   - Who gave to Paul to meet his needs?

9. Colossians 1:18 – *And he is the head of the body, the church. He is the beginning, the firstborn from the dead, that in everything he might be preeminent.*
   - Jesus is the head of what body?

10. Hebrews 10:24-25 – *And let us consider how to stir up one another to love and good works, [25] not neglecting to meet together, as is the habit of some, but encouraging one another, and all the more as you see the Day drawing near.*
    - What is the church to do?

APPLICATION

We can see from these verses that the church is not a building but a group of people who meet together, worship and teach, pray for one another, meet each other's needs, and stir up one another to love and good deeds. Jesus is the head of the church and gave himself up for her. Disciples of Jesus, aligned together as the church, demonstrate the many different ways God shows his wisdom to the world and to rulers and authorities in the heavenly places.

While each individual member of the body can show love and do good works, we do this best when we work as a team, as the church. Through teaching and Bible study, in large and small groups, we encourage each other to know God, learn to reject sin, minister to and meet each other's needs, and reach out to let the world know about Jesus and the good news. This is how disciples are made. And as each individual member becomes a strong disciple, the church becomes stronger and better able to reach the world with the gospel!

Here are some ways that you can become a greater part of a local church, besides just attendance on Sunday:

- **Become a consistent participant** in the large corporate gatherings and in a small group.
- **Serve in a ministry area of the church**. It can be simple, like serving on the greeter team.
- **Pray for someone in your church, or for a need or ministry the church has.** Write down below what you prayed for. Is there some way you can be the answer to your prayer by serving?
- **Begin to give financially** to the church. The guideline of the Bible is to give a tenth of your income.
- **If you have not yet been water baptized**, talk to your pastor or the person doing this material with you and see if you can set up a date to do so.

- **Participate in communion** whenever it is offered at your church.
- **Is there anything else that you sense that God wants you to do** for the church or for someone in church? Write it below and pray for God to help you be faithful.

Make a Disciple – One of the best ways to serve is to accompany another person through this *CrossWalk* study, especially someone who has come to know Jesus because of your prayers and sharing. Your discipler can help you if needed.

NEXT STEPS

Bible reading this week

If you are on schedule in your Bible reading you have finished the Gospel of John and the letters of 1 John, Ephesians, and Colossians. Congratulations if you have! If not, be sure to finish at least the Gospel of John right away. Consistency in reading your Bible is critical in your spiritual growth.

You can go on to the study guide *CrossFire* to continue growing in your relationship with Jesus and your knowledge of the Bible. *CrossFire* includes a Bible reading plan.

If you are not going to continue with *CrossFire* you can select another book of the Bible to read. Select a book in the New Testament. A good shorter book is Philippians. If you would like to read about the exciting story of the beginning of the church, then read the book of Acts. It's a longer book but you will love it!

Memorize

Matthew 16:18 – And I tell you, you are Peter, and on this rock I will build my church, and the gates of hell shall not prevail against it.

Prayer

Try to pray every day for 10-15 minutes using the ACTS acronym as a guide.

Adoration – Worship God for who he is: Creator, Almighty, Holy God, Savior, Redeemer, Father, Friend, etc. After you worship, take time to be quiet and listen.

Confession – Confess any sins and forgive anyone who may have sinned against you.

Thanksgiving – Thank God for His protection and provision in your life and in the world.

Supplication – Pray for your needs and the needs of others.

Practice the discipline of fasting a meal or a whole day whenever possible. Pray during the time you would normally be eating.

Share the Good News

Continue to seek opportunities to share your story about salvation or anything else that God is showing you.

Continue to pray for the people you listed to come to know Jesus. Expect that God will give your opportunities to share his good news with others!

You can make disciples in many nations!

If this book has been helpful to you, please consider helping it to be *printed and distributed in other nations of the world!*

Missio Global utilizes this book and the other books of the *Cross Series* for discipleship in several nations of the world. We currently want to add the following languages and nations:

- Portuguese in Brazil
- Swahili in Tanzania and East Africa
- Ukrainian in Ukraine

It typically costs about $2.50 per copy to print a book. At this rate, a **$100 contribution will print 40 copies of a book.** That is a tremendous investment in discipling the nations!

Please consider helping to *GO and make disciples* in the nations. Your tax deductible donation *(designate for Translation Fund)* can be made online at **missioglobal.com,**

or send by check to:

Missio Global
PO Box 17211
Asheville, NC 28816

THANK YOU!

ANSWERS

Step 1: Walking with God - Understanding Salvation

1. Mark 1:14-15 – Repent and believe the good news
2. John 5:11-13
   - God
   - In his Son
   - Whoever has the Son
   - Whoever does not have the Son
   - Know
   - Believe in the name of the Son of God
3. Romans 3:23 – No
4. Romans 6:23
   - The wage we receive for sin is death.
   - The free gift of God is eternal life through Jesus Christ our Lord.
5. Romans10:9-10
   - Confess with your mouth that Jesus is Lord and believe in your heart that God raised him from the dead.
   - Both are important because when you believe in your heart you are justified (legally you are declared not guilty) and when you confess with your mouth you are saved.
6. Ephesians 2:8-9
   - Grace
   - God
   - So that no one may boast
7. 1 John 3:9 – One born of God does not keep sinning because he is born of God and God's seed abides in him.

Application – The difference between feeling sorry for your sins and repenting of your sins is that when you repent you think differently and as a result repentance will affect the way you behave. Simply being sorry for your sins does not mean the way you think and act will change. Being sorry for your sins only means that you are sad about the consequences of your sin, but do not necessarily have an intention to change.

Step 2: Walking with Jesus - Understanding the Gospel

1. Colossians 1:15-22
    - Jesus is the image of the invisible God, the firstborn of all creation (verse 15). He is before all things, and in him all things hold together (verse 17). He is the head of the church, the beginning, the first born from the dead (verse 18).
    - By him all things were created, in heaven and on earth, visible and invisible, whether thrones or dominions or rulers or authorities – all things were created through him and for him.
    - All the fullness of God.
    - He reconciled to himself all things, whether on earth or in heaven, making peace by the blood of his cross.
    - We were alienated and hostile in mind; we did evil deeds.
    - To present us holy and blameless and above reproach before him (God).
2. Philippians 2:3-11
    - Count others as more significant; look to their interests.
    - He did not count equality with God a thing to be grasped (to be held onto). He emptied himself, taking the form of a servant, and was born as a man. As a man he became obedient to the point of death, and suffered death on a cross.
    - God has highly exalted him and bestowed on him the name that is above every name. At the name of Jesus every knee will bow in heave, on earth and under the earth, and every tongue will confess that Jesus Christ is Lord.

Step 3: Walking as an Ambassador - Sharing the Good News

1. 2 Corinthians 5:18-21
    - The ministry of reconciliation.
    - God reconciled the world to himself through Christ. Reconciliation means there was a break in a relationship and something was done to restore it. Sin broke our relationship with God and Jesus' death on the cross restored the relationship. He reconciled those who trust and obey Jesus to right relationship with God.
    - God makes his appeal through us—those who follow Jesus. The title he gives us is Christ's ambassadors.
2. Mark 5:18-20 (full story is Mark 5:1-20)
    - Jesus told the man to go home to his own people and tell them how much the Lord had done for him, and how he had mercy on him. The result was that all the people he told were amazed.
3. Mark 16:15 (full context is Mark16:15-20)
    - Jesus told his disciples to go into all the world and preach the gospel (good news) to all creation. In order for people to be reconciled to God they need to believe in Jesus. The only way for them to believe is for someone to tell them. (See Romans 10:14)
    - I can obey this command by sharing my testimony, telling them about Jesus, inviting them to church or event. (Add anything else)

Step 4: Walking in the Word - Knowing God through the Bible

1. Hebrews 4:12
    - Living and active.
    - A sword pierces and divides joints and marrow. The word pierces and divides soul and spirit, discerning the thoughts and intentions of the heart.

2. Psalm 119:105 – A lamp will light up and show the path and where you can put your feet. God's word shows us how we are to walk with God, love him, obey him.
3. Psalm 119:130 – Light equals understanding in this passage. It gives understanding to the simple.
4. Psalm 119:133 – No sin will rule over us.
5. Psalm 119:160 – God's word is true and endures forever. (It means I can trust God and his word because it is truth and never changes. Add anything it means to you.)
6. Isaiah 40:8 – They wither and fall. The Word stands forever.
7. Isaiah 55:10-11 – The Word of God will not return empty, it will accomplish the purpose God desires, and succeed in the thing for which He sent it.
8. Matthew 4:4 – Our lives should be sustained by every word that comes from the mouth of God.
9. Luke 11:28 – Hear the word and obey it.

Application – It penetrates and judges our thoughts and attitudes; it shows us who God is and how we are to live; it gives us understanding; it keeps sin from ruling over us; it sustains us more than food; we are blessed when we hear and obey it.

Step 5: Walking in Prayer - Talking and Listening to God

1. Exodus 33:11a – God spoke to Moses face to face, as a man speaks to his friend.
2. Psalm 66:17-20 – God listens.
3. Psalm 102:17 – He responds to their prayers.
4. Proverbs 15:8 – The prayer of the upright.
5. Matthew 21:22 – You receive whatever you ask for in prayer.
6. Philippians 4:6 – We are to pray and make our requests known to God.
7. Colossians 4:2 – By being watchful in prayer, with thanksgiving.

8. James 5:13-16 – We are to pray all the time – when we are suffering, sick, have sinned or are happy. We pray so that we (or others) can be forgiven or healed.
9. Acts 10:30-31 – God

Step 6: Walking with the Holy Spirit - Knowing the Power of God

1. Psalm 104:29-30 – Things are created and renewed.
2. Romans 8:1-2 – We are set free from the law of sin and death. (Note: The law of sin and death is that when we sin we die – we are separated from God. The law of the Spirit is that when we receive Jesus' sacrifice as payment for our sins we are no longer separated from God. Instead, we are set free, and the Holy Spirit comes and lives within us.)
3. Acts 1:8 – To be His witness everywhere on earth.
4. Matthew 12:28 – By the Spirit of God.
   1 Corinthians 12:8-11 – Word of wisdom, word of knowledge, faith, gifts of healing, working of miracles, prophecy, distinguishing between spirits, different kinds of tongues, interpretation of tongues.
5. Galatians 5:16, 22-23 – You will not gratify the desires of the flesh. Love, joy, peace, patience, kindness, goodness, faithfulness, gentleness, and self-control are produced.
   Romans 8:5, 14 –They are children of God.
6. 1 Corinthians 6:11 – By the Spirit of our God.
7. 2 Peter 1:20-21 – By God as they were carried along by the Holy Spirit.
8. Romans 14:7 – By righteousness, peace, and joy in the Holy Spirit.
9. 1 John 4:13 – Because He has given us His Spirit.
10. John 14:26 – By teaching you all things and bringing to your remembrance all that he said.
    John 16:13 – He will guide you into all truth because he will reveal to you what he hears from God.
11. Ephesians 4:1-3 – We maintain the unity of the Spirit in the bond of peace.

12. Acts 7:51 – We can resist the Holy Spirit
    Ephesians 4:30 – We can grieve the Holy Spirit.
    1 Thessalonians 5:19 – We can quench the Holy Spirit.
    Acts 5:3 – We can lie to the Holy Spirit.
    Luke 12:10 – We can blaspheme against the Holy Spirit.

Step 7: Walking in Freedom - Fighting from a Place of Victory

1. Lies and Strongholds – 2 Corinthians 10:2-5
   - The world fights using worldly weapons, strong words and threats.
   - Followers of Jesus fight with weapons that have divine power to demolish strongholds like arguments and pretensions that set themselves up against the knowledge of God. They fight taking every thought captive to make it obedient to Christ.
   - A stronghold is arguments, opinions or thoughts that oppose God's wisdom, knowledge and authority. It is a lie. You tear it down through the truth found in the Bible. Reading the Bible and praying, alone and with others, as well as confessing sin, asking forgiveness, and forgiving others are ways to tear down strongholds in your life.
2. Deception – Colossians 2:6-8
   - We are to live rooted and built up in Christ, strengthened in the faith, and overflowing with thankfulness.
   - Worldly philosophy is hollow and deceptive because it depends on human tradition and the elemental spiritual forces of the world rather than on Christ.
   - Practical ways to learn truth is through the Bible. Praying, going to church, and spending time with others who know Jesus can help me learn truth. But I also need to put what I learn into practice—I need to obey.

3. Temptation – Luke 4:9-14
   - Satan challenged Jesus' deity, tempting Jesus to glorify himself. He also quoted scripture—Psalm 91:11-12. Jesus responded with scripture, "Do not put the Lord your God to the test."
   - He was quoting scripture: Deuteronomy 8:3, 6:13, and 6:16.
   - Jesus left the wilderness in the **power** of the Spirit.
   - Know what the Bible says and speak it; say no to sin— even people. Pray and surround myself with people who I can learn from who know Jesus. Add any other helpful responses.

Step 8: Walking with the Church - Knowing God through Community

1. Matthew 16:18 – Jesus
2. Acts 11:19-27 – The church in Jerusalem; the church in Antioch
3. Acts 12:5 – The church
4. Acts 15:1-4 – The church in Antioch; the church in Jerusalem
5. Ephesians 3:10 –The church; to make it known to the rulers and authorities in the heavenly places.
6. 1 Timothy 3:14-15
   - A household of God, a pillar and foundation of the truth.
   - A pillar supports the roof and walls of a structure and a foundation supports a pillar, allowing it to stand stronger and higher.
   - The Church is called to have a solid foundation and stand strong, supporting, like a pillar, the truth of the gospel of Jesus Christ.
7. Ephesians 5:25 – Jesus gave himself up for the church.
8. Philippians 4:15 – The church in Philippi
9. Colossians 1:18 – The church

10. Hebrews 10:24-25 – Stir up one another to love and good works, not neglect to meet together, and encourage one another.

ABOUT THE AUTHORS

Scott and Sherri Dalton serve as the International Directors for Missio Global. They have over 30 years of experience in church planting and ministry leadership training, including over fourteen years in Brazil where they planted a church and launched the first international Missio Global School of Ministry. Scott and Sherri both have doctorate degrees from Summit Bible College. They currently live in the United States and have five adult children and six grandchildren.

ABOUT MISSIO GLOBAL

Missio Global prepares ministry workers in partnership with churches worldwide by providing resources for making disciples, training leaders, and planting churches. Our vision is to empower thousands of churches worldwide to equip workers to reach and disciple millions of people for Christ.

MISSIO GLOBAL SCHOOL OF MINISTRY

The Missio Global School of Ministry is a partnership between Missio Global and churches around the world. This school is a valuable one or three-year training program that churches can use to equip their members and develop emerging leaders.

The host local church is the laboratory where the students serve and complete ministry projects. In this setting, the students learn from the experience and wisdom of their church leaders. The goal of the school is to create a fruitful learning community in the local church that will develop future leaders and ultimately plant new churches.

Churches in numerous nations are hosting a Missio Global School of Ministry, with the curriculum currently in seven languages.

For information about hosting a Missio Global School of Ministry in your church, visit missioglobal.com

THE CROSS SERIES

The Cross Series is a book series for Christian growth focusing on discipleship and the initial stages of leadership development. The material is best used in a one-on-one discipleship relationship or in micro-groups of up to four people. The Cross Series is designed as a growth track that leads to the church-based Missio Global School of Ministry. It can also be used as valuable equipping material for general Christian discipleship. Titles include:

CrossWalk – Vital Steps in Your Walk With God
CrossFire – A New Way of Living (Books 1 & 2)

For information on quantity discounts, contact us at
team@missioglobal.org

www.ingramcontent.com/pod-product-compliance
Lightning Source LLC
Chambersburg PA
CBHW071930020426
42331CB00010B/2805